Innocence Ran Naked Down the Street

poems

HOPE NISIVOCCIA

Paperback: ISBN 979-8-9922075-0-7
E-book: ISBN 979-8-9922075-2-1
Audiobook: ISBN 979-8-9922075-1-4

First Paperback edition: May 2025

Edited by Marie Deer
Cover Design by Miladinka Milic
Layout by Niokoba

Printed by What Hope Can Bring Press in the USA

To Ms. Florin—my 1st and 4th Grade Teacher

*Thank you for encouraging and supporting my love of writing.
I still have the two grammar books you bought
me in fourth grade.
I will forever appreciate you.*

Table of Contents

I

Walking Wounded

"They don't hurt anymore," she said.
"They're just scars."

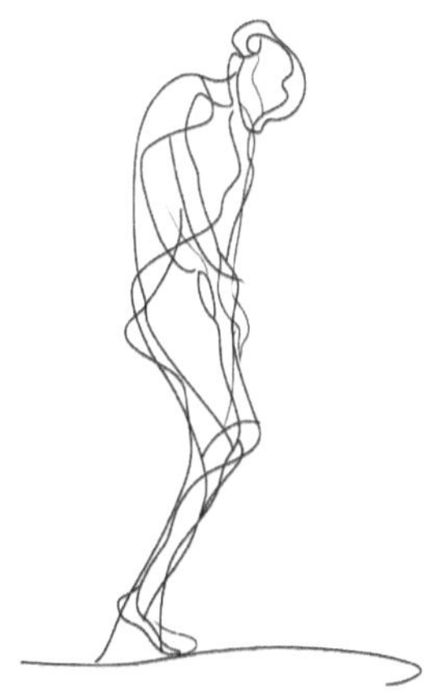

You Stole It from Me

You left my heart dangling from my chest
by the cords
your handprint embedded in my breast
imprinted in my left cheek.
You stole it from me.

My voice box left empty
my mind filled with scarred memories
my eyes scabbed over so that I see red
even if I am awake
the brightest sun is black.
You stole it from me.

Innocence ran naked down the street,
screaming "Look! Look at what he did! Help me, please!"
Purity nestled herself in her arms
and cried herself to sleep
dreaming of shriveled flowers, sun-scorched lilies.
You stole it from me.

Now,
Trust bleeds
Hope and Faith hold hands and weep
and Love screams
as they watch me f
                    a
                      l
                        l
                            apart

at the seams

My soul left
in an unrecognizable
state

The "Misunderstanding"

This is a "misunderstanding" I can't understand
Is to love—to hate?
Why do young breasts feel an adult hand?

An imprint that remains and
burns so Love aches, Trust shakes
This is a "misunderstanding" I can't understand

My nakedness no longer my own
My soul left in an unrecognizable state
Is to love—to hate?

Teardrops like grains of sand
Fall from eyes shut with pain, overwhelmed by this fate
This is a "misunderstanding" I can't understand

Who are you? Who am I?—questions this plight demands
Was our time together and affection just bait?
Is to love—to hate?

Our relationship—a twisted, stretched, popped rubber band
Are you my guardian or some kind of mate?
I can't understand, I won't understand
Love is not hate.

Not Your Dumping Ground

I've taken on your pain
played the role you wanted me to play—
your sacrificial lamb
your punching bag
the object of your wrath—

But now I've figured out it's not my job
to be the tissue for your sob
the crutch for your limp
your wrongdoings' eclipse
your dumping ground

I believed you when you said it was my fault
With Doubt, I wrestled and fought
When I was told I was too sensitive or whacked—
I became Loneliness's most resentful companion

How long was I supposed to suffocate
while you breathed all the air?
How long was I supposed to hide
while you paraded in the open with your lies?
How long was I supposed to stay
in prison for your crimes?

Read the sign BIG and **bold**,
erected on the fringes of my soul—
E-NOUGH!
I AM *NOT*
YOUR DUMPING GROUND.

Hurting

You looked Innocence in the face
and hurt it
and what did you gain?
Your soul turned black
emboldened with red
hues of pride

You sowed pain—
now you reap your own destruction
But did you do what you did
because you were hurt as a kid?
That doesn't make it right,
but I know, without love,
things die

Did you start to die
when they hurt you that way?
What made you into
this
monster—
degenerate and carnal?

You looked Innocence in the face
and hurt it
because you
you yourself
were hurting

I'm triggered
—not unsafe

Triggered

When the feeling grips me
I'm terrified—yes, terrified—I say
Then I remember:
Oh, I'm triggered—not unsafe

Remembering, my body
freezes in pain
paralyzed by shock
stunned, in a daze

When the feeling grips me
I'm terrified—terrified—even today
Then I remember:
I'm triggered—not unsafe

My heartbeat racing me
up, to the moon
Helplessness swooping in,
pecking me down down down

Sometimes I'm gripped by that feeling
And terrified—terrified—yes, throughout the day
So I keep reminding myself:
I'm triggered—not unsafe

Lord, Will You Listen?

I have a lot to say,
and so I pray—
Lord, will you listen?

I shout to the seas, and they shoot me with spray
The earth keeps turning, won't give me the time of day
I plead to the stars; they wink and twinkle—
Are they just smirking?

I have a lot to say,
and so I pray.

Is the universe laughing so hard that I can't hear it?
Do the seas spray me in jest or are they wailing with me?
Is the turning earth just trying to bring me the sun?
Are those winking, twinkling stars in fact blinking,
wet with tears that glisten instead of run?

Heard or ignored,
attended to or abandoned,
I have a lot to say,
and so I pray.

To you, God,
who knows the stars by name,
tilts the Earth,
and silences the waves,

I pray.

Questions

Where were you, Lord,
when Innocence's veil was torn?

Did you just look on
as my dreams were ripped apart
and scattered,
my sense of self shattered?

Am I now only a heap of pain,
reeking of shame?
Or is there more to who I am
than what he did to me?

Do I pull away from you
because I don't understand
or do I trust you—
do I trust your plan?

Who can give beauty
for the ashes,
making all things
new?

Who,
but you?

II

Wounds to Wisdom

The Push and the Pull

How is it that I get caught in these waves—
tossed about, shaken, beaten till I'm dazed?
With salty water tearing at my throat,
desperate and dejected, I choke
Wet and drenched in the shame
of being too weak to say no,
I wash up on the shore hurt, exposed

This tug-of-war that poses as love
leaves me face down in the sand,
my heart covered in burns
from friction when dragged
Mistaking intensity for intimacy
leaves me drenched in sweat,
chasing an illusion
exhausted with regret

I am tired of these games
that two unripe, unsure people play
depending on each other to fulfill
longings that only God can satiate

The push and the pull—
the tug-of-war
of hurting, broken souls
The push and the pull—
when will I find rest in Christ alone?

I open my eyes
to find myself exposed—
scars of abuse unveiled
to the biting cold
I cover my ears
but still hear the silent sobs of a shattered soul
I close my eyes
and dreams of dying become my fantasy

Perhaps if I were dead
this agony would cease.

The push and the pull—
the tug-of-war
for hurting, broken souls
The push and the pull—
when will my life be Christ's alone?
The push and the pull—
who will win this battle for my soul?

My Heart's Lament

My heart clutches a dead dream
Lord, will you salve this terrible sting?
He sees *her* and not me—he wants *her* for his queen

The dam of hope breaks and my tears start to stream
From shock to confusion, my jilted self swings
My heart clutches a dead dream

Remember our laughter? Our faces beamed
Our conversation—deep, engrossing, supreme
I wanted much more—my desire grew wings
Lord, will you salve this terrible sting?

Will a man ever love me?—my doubting heart teems
My hope loses grip and hangs from a string
My heart clutches a dead dream

Alone again now with the God who redeems
To You, O Lord, my broken heart I bring
Lord, will you salve this impossible sting?

You know all my struggles. With you, I am seen
You grasp me, you hear me, you know me, my King!
My heart mourns the death of a dream
My Lord will salve this rejected heart's sting.

Sorry

You wanted me,
but I didn't know me,
so I couldn't give me away

You gave your whole heart,
and I was unswayed

What you saw was a facade—
a disguise for the unfinished parts of me,
and as you sought me out,
I continued to encase them behind glass
like ancient art

I broke your heart
as you reached for mine
I couldn't love you—even with time
so frustration grew
ripping us apart—
we were finished from the start

I think about us
I think about you
then I think about me
and all I can say is . . .
I'm sorry

The lessons
are mine to keep

Lessons

It's time to move on
but the lessons are mine to keep
treasure and hold close
breathe in deep
bury in the crevices of my heart
as I watch you depart—
your back turned to me

Thank you for leaving behind
these memories
love etched in my mind
the most beautiful design—
it fades, but the lessons are mine
to keep

You were not the message
but the messenger
and now that you have brought me
what I needed
it's time to move on
to bless another soul
as you have blessed mine

So why do I weep?
The tears sting my eyes
as I say goodbye
and cherish the lessons
you left behind

To Be Loved

I gave my heart to someone
who never wanted it
As I laid it in his hand,
he grimaced, "What is this for?"
and chucked it like garbage

Jesus,
Will you be the one that I need,
hold me and console me?
Will you love me as the broken woman that I am
and with your love,
heal wounds, deep and aching?

Back in my own lap again, my heart
thumps with pain and disillusionment
What's to blame for the shame that flushes my face?
My desperation? My cluelessness?
Or just my quiet willingness to be debased?

Jesus,
Will you be the one that I need,
who will love me in spite of my poor choices
and the crooked roads toward love I used to take?

All I ever wanted was to be loved,
but somehow I learned the game wrong
and got played by Jokers,
Crazy Eights, and Evil Spades—
Who's to blame?

Jesus,
Dear God, show me the way!
Lord and Savior,
wrap me in your grace!
Will you be my sacred treasure?
Please, please, may I bask in your glory forever?

Back in my own lap again, my heart
thumps with rage and disillusionment
Who's to blame?

Lord, I know it is a lot to ask
from a sinful girl like me,
but knowing who You are,
I dare to ask. I dare to dream.

All I ever wanted was to be loved,
but somehow I learned the game wrong—
When he barged in setting off the alarms
I covered my ears and cringed
but the deafening blare within never stops

Lord, I am ready to shed the sackcloth of shame
and accept your garment of grace
I gave Sin, the World, and Satan
a thousand yesterdays
but today is when you are finally
most glorified in my life
and I am redeemed.

You melt away
my shame

What Brings Me Peace

Dedicated to My Heavenly Dad

What brings me peace
is knowing that you care
knowing that no matter what
you'll always be there

You see me as I am—
broken and in shambles—
and love every piece of me
like every piece is valuable

You melt away my shame
with your loving gaze
while I struggle with the words
I once dared not to say

What brings me peace
is knowing that you care
knowing that no matter what
you'll always be there

III

RESURRECTING DREAMS

"And I got this scar when I fell . . ."
"What were you doing when you fell?"
"I was reaching for my dreams . . ."

I Got Dreams

I got dreams
that I can't seem to get off the ground
The engine rattles,
but there's no movement—
just that funny sound

These wings are full of dents
and I feel like a clown
stuck in the pilot's seat, trying
to get this thing off the ground!

I'm engulfed by emotion—
billows of commotion
fog up my view

Do I need a license to fly this thing?
Is desire enough permission to spread my wings?

The engine rattles,
but there's no movement—
just that gurgly sound

When this thing gets flying,
I pray it soars
instead of just hovering
above the ground

I got dreams

Fear Will Feast on My Dreams

Desire unfulfilled aches
What can I do but wait?
Will thrashing and whining
change my fate?

I rage at God,
that only prolongs my pain—
desire unfulfilled aches
What can I do but wait?

Father, what does waiting mean?
Is it just flat emptiness
or a time to plan and dream?

Are my dreams out there ready,
opportunities for me to seize?
Or needs I have to meet,
moments I must create?

What if I delay and fixate on doubt?
Fear will feast on my dreams
and Regret will glean the crumbs
of my desire

What will be left of me?
The remnants of a bitter woman
drawing from her deck of excuses
If only—If not for . . .

Yes, desire unfulfilled aches
Why do I delay?
My lack of faith has kept me in this state

Desire unfulfilled aches—
but if I just walk,
won't God lead the way?
C'mon! I tell myself, be brave!

This pep talk has lasted an hour—
am I now filled with power?
Is this who I am,
just a dreamer?

I remember God's promises
and pray
I choose to trust
and obey

If I just walk,
won't God lead the way?

I wiggle my toes
I bend my leg—
action is one step away!

It Means So Much to Me I Could Break

Desire swells—hampered, contained,
shaking, rattling its cage of fear
It means so much to me I could break

If I go after life with abandon,
will I end up with empty hands?
If I drink deeply of pleasure,
feel the heartbeat of passion,
experience life unrationed—
will I explode
going from starvation to obesity?
It means so much to me I could break

Life gushing, rushing,
flowing, brightly glowing
It means so much to me I could break

From this standstill to start moving—
it means so much to me I could break!
From this emptiness to be fulfilled—
it means so much to me I could break!

Desire swells—hampered, contained,
shaking, rattling its cage of fear
The door flings open—
Do I dare
step out?

From my cage, I run
my heart like drumbeats
feet strumming the ground—
It meant so much to me
I pushed—
and broke free!

Epilogue

This Poem Is Not Just for Me but for Women like Me

This poem is not just for me
but for women like me—
Women
living in private perpetual pain
until their hearts go numb
Women
whose trust
has been cropped, crushed, and crippled
before it could blossom
into love

This poem is for women
who soak their pillows at night with tears
and yet, face the world the next day as though fearless
Women
who wear the mask of resilience
but are still little broken girls inside
terror-struck
at what their daddies did to them

This poem is for women
who think the only way
to rid themselves of Misery's company
is to dine with Death
and so entertain thoughts of suicide
and even attempt—

This poem is for women
who master survival
but fail at living
Women
who passionately give
to everyone and everything
but not themselves—
never ourselves

This poem is for women
who finally
break down—
in sorrow
in pain
in need
of something, someone to show them the way

This poem is for women
who question God
Is He there?
Does He love them?
Does He care?

This poem is for women
who lie dying in their own pool of blood,
famished
by the World's empty promises,
tarnished
by the stain of sin,
ravished
by Satan
who runs away laughing—
flaunting, dangling their innocence

This poem is not just for me
but for women like me—
Women
who know
harassment, helplessness
Women
confused and condemned,
disillusioned and spiritually dead—

Until
God shows up
and cries,
"LIVE!"

REFLECTION